CONTENTS

INTRODUCTION

Chinese envoy Zhang Qian leaves Emperor Wu of Han around 130 BCE. His travels in Central Asia help open the east–west trade route known as the Silk Road.

Throughout time, humans have been tempted to travel in order to find food and places to live. Sometimes curiosity and a sense of adventure played a part too. The first explorers were the prehistoric peoples that spread out from Africa from two million years ago. By around 10,000 years ago, people had settled all over the world. Some had travelled by foot across land bridges that are now under the sea, such as the ones that connected Asia and North America, and Britain with mainland Europe. Others crossed the oceans on rafts or in simple dugout canoes.

As civilisations arose, people continued to explore. The Greeks settled not only mainland Greece and the Greek islands, but also parts of Turkey and colonies around the Mediterranean as far west as France. Across the world, empires began to take shape as people discovered new lands. The vast Roman empire stretched from Spain in the west to Syria in the east. When it collapsed in the late 400s, smaller European states formed, each with their own interests.

Until the discovery of the New World in the late 1400s, European ideas about what the world looked like were mostly based on hearsay. The Fra Mauro map (left), one of the greatest medieval European maps of the known world, was made around 1450 by a Venetian monk called Fra Mauro. It shows remarkable detail, but half the world is missing and the south is at the top!

The Greek geographer Pytheas was from Massalia (present-day Marseille in southern France). Around 325 BCE he explored northwestern Europe, including Britain (right).

A BRIEF ILLUSTRATED
HISTORY of
EXPLORATION

CLARE HIBBERT
&
DAVID WEST

raintree

a Capstone company — publishers for children

Published by Raintree, an imprint of Capstone Global Library Limited, 2017.
Raintree is an imprint of Capstone Global Library Limited, a company incorporated in England and Wales
having its registered office at 264 Banbury Road, Oxford, OX2 7DY –
Registered company number: 6695582
www.raintree.co.uk
myorders@raintree.co.uk

Designed and illustrated by David West
Text by Clare Hibbert
Editor Brenda Haugen
Produced by
David West Children's Books, 6 Princeton Court, 55 Felsham Road, London SW15 1AZ
Printed and bound in Malaysia

ISBN: 978-1-4747-2706-8 (hardcover)
ISBN: 978-1-4747-2712-9 (paperback)
20 19 18 17 16
10 9 8 7 6 5 4 3 2 1

British Library Cataloguing in Publication Data
A full catalogue record for this book is available from the British Library.

Every effort has been made to contact copyright holders of material reproduced in this book. Any
omissions will be rectified in subsequent printings if notice is given to the publisher.

EARLY OCEAN EXPLORERS
750 – 1433

THE VIKINGS LIVED AROUND THE COASTS OF SCANDINAVIA (PRESENT-DAY DENMARK, NORWAY AND SWEDEN). THEY FARMED, FISHED AND BECAME SKILFUL SHIPBUILDERS. THEY TOOK TO THE SEAS IN THEIR LONGSHIPS TO RAID OR SETTLE OTHER LANDS. THEY ALSO ESTABLISHED A TRADING NETWORK ACROSS EUROPE AS FAR AS ASIA.

VIKING VOYAGES

Leif Erikson — GREENLAND — Early voyages — ICELAND — SCANDINAVIA — Erik the Red — VINLAND — Bjarni Herjólfsson

Leif Erikson sights the coast of North America.

Only the coastal areas of Scandinavia were fit for settlement. No one ventured inland because it was so cold and hostile. Instead, people sailed to other lands. From around 750 BCE, the Vikings began to raid western Europe and earned a fearsome reputation. But many were just looking for enough fertile farmland to support their families. Viking explorers settled in northern Scotland

Vikings sailing to Greenland

on Orkney and Shetland. They also discovered the Faroe Islands, Iceland and Greenland, where Erik the Red founded a Viking settlement in 985 AD.

A year earlier the explorer Bjarni Herjólfsson had been the first European to sight North America.

Erik the Red's son Leif Erikson was the first to land there. He established a colony that he called Vinland in Newfoundland, Canada, around 1000 AD.

Zheng He

Muslim-born Zheng He was only 10 years old when he was captured by Chinese soldiers in 1381 and sent to serve the Prince of Yan. Later, that prince became emperor of all China, and Zheng was his trusted advisor and admiral. Between 1405 and 1433, Zheng captained seven expeditions across the Indian Ocean. He produced maps and charts and brought back many exotic treasures, including a giraffe – a present for the emperor from the Sultan of Bengal.

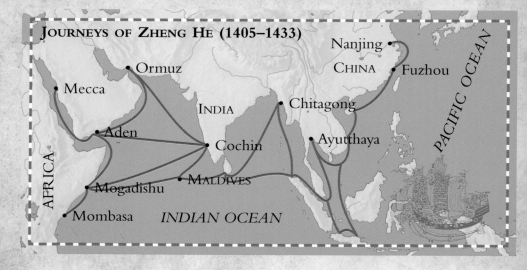

JOURNEYS OF ZHENG HE (1405–1433)

Nanjing • CHINA • Fuzhou • Ormuz • Mecca • INDIA • Chitagong • Aden • Cochin • Ayutthaya • MALDIVES • Mogadishu • Mombasa • INDIAN OCEAN • AFRICA • PACIFIC OCEAN

ENVOYS, MERCHANTS AND TRAVELLERS
300 – 1354

From the Middle Ages, the reasons for travel became more political. Emperors and kings sent out envoys (messengers) to tell of their power, call in tribute or establish new trade routes. The Christian Church was growing too as more people were converted to its beliefs. It built churches across Europe and beyond.

In 1245 Pope Innocent IV sent four missions to ask the Mongols to convert to Christianity. Here, Ascelin of Lombardy presents a letter from the pope to Baiju, a Mongol commander in Persia.

Christian missionaries were around from the early Middle Ages. Ulfilas from central Turkey converted the German Visigoths in the 300s AD. Patrick, a bishop in Roman Britain, introduced Christianity to Ireland in the early 400s AD. Over time, the Church in Rome became the greatest power in western Europe.

From around 1000, holy wars took place between European Christians and Muslims in the Middle East, who had captured Jerusalem. Europeans from all levels of society fought in these wars, called Crusades by the Christians, who wanted to claim back Jerusalem.

Beyond the Middle East lay the vast Mongol empire, which stretched into what is now China. Many explorers wrote of their travels east along the Silk Road. Visitors to the court of the Mongol ruler, or Great Khan, included the Flemish missionary William of Rubruck in 1254 and the Venetian merchant Marco Polo, who made his fortune travelling in central Asia from 1271 to 1295.

Marco Polo's travels in central Asia with his father and uncle last 24 years.

Ibn Battuta
In 1325 Ibn Battuta went on a pilgrimage to Mecca from his home, Tangiers in north Africa. While in Mecca, he dreamt about travelling on the back of a giant bird, which he believed was a sign from God. Ibn Battuta decided to visit every Muslim country in the world. Just 20 years old at the start of his journey, he travelled for 30 years and visited 40 countries across Africa and Asia. He wrote a book about his travels called the *Rihla* (*The Journey*).

Journeys of Ibn Battuta (1325–1354)

Constantinople · Black Sea · Caspian Sea · ASIA · Beijing
Mediterranean Sea · Tangiers · Basra · Delhi · CHINA
Alexandria · Jeddah · Mecca · INDIA
Timbuktu · AFRICA · MALDIVES · SRI LANKA
Mombasa · INDIAN OCEAN
Kilwa

EXPLORATIONS OF THE PORTUGUESE
1418 – 1543

THE EUROPEAN AGE OF EXPLORATION BEGAN IN THE EARLY 1400S WHEN PORTUGUESE SAILORS VENTURED OUT INTO THE ATLANTIC OCEAN. THEY EXPLORED THE WESTERN COAST OF AFRICA. WITH ENCOURAGEMENT FROM THEIR PRINCE, HENRY THE NAVIGATOR, THEY SET THEIR SIGHTS ON DISCOVERING A SEA ROUTE TO ASIA AND ITS PRECIOUS SILK, SPICES AND JEWELS.

Henry the Navigator (1394–1460)

Prince Henry of Portugal earned the nickname Henry the Navigator because of his support for seafaring and exploration. In 1418 he set up the first school of oceanic navigation at Sagres, Portugal, which provided training in navigation, cartography and science. This led to the discovery of the uninhabited islands of Madeira in 1419 and the Azores in 1427, both of which were claimed for Portugal. At that time, no European had sailed down the western coast of Africa beyond Cape Bojador, which was known for its strong currents and storms.

Bartolomeu Dias's caravels – the São Cristóvão *and* São Pantaleão *– sail towards the Cape of Good Hope in 1488. The fleet also had one support ship.*

Vasco da Gama lands in Calicut (now Kozhikode) in 1498.

Henry sent out expeditions to go beyond Cape Bojador. This was achieved in 1434 by the explorer Gil Eannes.

Near the end of his life, Henry the Navigator funded two expeditions by the Venetian explorer, Alvise da Cadamosto. In 1455 Cadamosto reached the mouth of the Gambia River. In 1456 he sailed up the Gambia River to the Geba River. He also claimed to have discoverd the Cape Verde Islands.

Explorer's ships

Ships had simple sails from earliest times. The Egyptians, Greeks, Phoenicians and Romans all used them to harness the power of the wind. Over time, shipbuilders improved their designs, developing particular shapes and groupings of sails to suit different conditions.

The Portuguese developed the caravel in the 1400s. Lightweight, manoeuvrable and speedy, it had lateen (triangular) sails on its two masts. The advantage of triangular sails was that the ship could sail closer to the wind than a ship with square sails. The ship also had a shallow keel (hull) so it could sail inland up rivers. However, the design also had disadvantages. Its relatively small size could not accommodate much cargo and limited the crew to no more than around 20 sailors.

First appearing in the mid-1400s, the caravel aided Portuguese exploration.

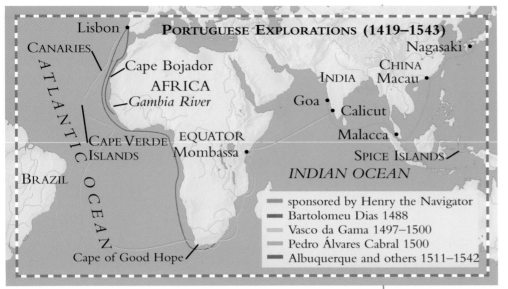

PORTUGUESE EXPLORATIONS (1419–1543)

Lisbon
CANARIES
Cape Bojador
AFRICA
Gambia River
Nagasaki
CHINA
INDIA   Macau
Goa
Calicut
Malacca
CAPE VERDE   EQUATOR
ISLANDS   Mombassa
SPICE ISLANDS
BRAZIL   *INDIAN OCEAN*
ATLANTIC OCEAN
Cape of Good Hope

— sponsored by Henry the Navigator
— Bartolomeu Dias 1488
— Vasco da Gama 1497–1500
— Pedro Álvares Cabral 1500
— Albuquerque and others 1511–1542

When Henry the Navigator died in 1460, the Portuguese lost interest in African exploration until the reign of Henry's great-nephew, John II (1481–1495). In 1481 John sent a dozen ships to São Jorge da Mina (present-day Elmina in Ghana)

to build a fort and trading post. Two years later Diogo Cao discovered the Congo River. In 1488 Bartolomeu Dias made history by being the first to round the Cape of Good Hope on the southern tip of Africa.

The Portuguese empire grew under John II's successor, Manuel I. In 1498 Vasco da Gama finally fulfilled Henry the Navigator's dream when he discovered a sea route to India and landed in Calicut. Another Portuguese admiral, Pedro Álvares Cabral headed west across the Atlantic. He discovered and claimed Brazil for Portugal in 1500, then continued on around Africa to India, a voyage that touched on four continents.

Afonso de Albuquerque was one of the great figures of the age. He was the first European to enter the Persian Gulf or sail in the Red Sea. He also added to Portugal's lands in southeast Asia. He claimed Goa in 1510, Malacca in 1511 and the Spice Islands (present-day Maluku Islands in Indonesia), with their nutmeg, mace, pepper and cloves, in 1512.

In 1500 Pedro Álvares Cabral becomes the first European to set foot in South America as he claims Brazil for Portugal.

Afonso de Albuquerque (around 1453–1515)

Navigation

The Chinese invented the magnetic compass in the 1000s, but European sailors did not adopt it for centuries. From the 1400s, the Portuguese led the way in mapping currents and trade winds. Seafarers learned how to work out their latitude using a compass, a cross-staff or astrolabe and simple nautical charts. The cross-staff had been around in ancient times, but the astrolabe was new. Soon, navigators could also use an hourglass to work out their longitude.

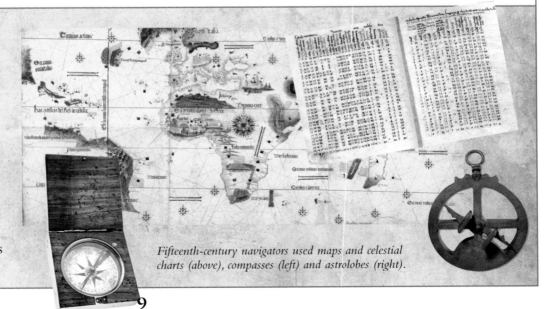

Fifteenth-century navigators used maps and celestial charts (above), compasses (left) and astrolabes (right).

A NEW WORLD
1492 – 1542

THE NEW WORLD OF THE AMERICAS WAS UNKNOWN TO THE OLD WORLD OF EUROPE AND ASIA UNTIL THE FIRST ENCOUNTER IN 1492. THE VERY IDEA OF SAILING WEST ACROSS THE ATLANTIC WAS BOTH DANGEROUS AND DARING. BUT ONE MAN BELIEVED HE COULD REACH ASIA BY THAT ROUTE – AND HIS OBSESSION LED TO THE GREATEST DISCOVERY IN THE HISTORY OF EXPLORATION.

Christopher Columbus (around 1451–1506)

The Genoese captain, Christopher Columbus, believed that he could travel west to China and India via Japan. He managed to convince the king and queen of Spain to fund his trip, but he had calculated Earth's circumference at 20 per cent smaller than its true size.

Columbus's fleet of three ships – the *Santa María*, the *Pinta* and the *Niña* – set sail from Palos in Spain on 3 August 1492. Three months later, on 11 October 1492, the crew sighted land. But it was not Asia. The fleet had arrived on an island in the Bahamas. Believing it to be near the East Indies, Columbus called the inhabitants 'Indians'. He explored the coasts of the two largest Caribbean islands, Cuba and Hispaniola (present-day Haiti and Dominican Republic). Friendly native people met them and even supplied the crews with fresh food and water. But on Christmas Eve the *Santa María* ran aground off Hispaniola.

Christopher Columbus steps onto an island in the present-day Bahamas and claims it for Spain, naming it San Salvador. He is the first person from the Old World to reach the New World since the Vikings.

Conquistadors

The Spanish were quickly established in the Caribbean. Soon they were exploring mainland Central and North America and claiming it for Spain. These Spanish conquerors were known as the conquistadors.

Hernán Cortés

Cortés arrived in Hispaniola in 1504 at age 18 and made his fortune. In 1519 he led the third Spanish expedition into what is now Mexico. His aim was to conquer the Aztecs.

When Cortés reached Tenochtitlan, the Aztec capital, the people thought he was a god. He captured the Aztec ruler, Moctezuma II, and defeated the empire by 1521. Cortés became governor of the new territory.

Pedro Arias Dávila

Dávila was 70 years old when he led one of the largest Spanish expeditions to the New World. In 1524 he founded Panama City.

Cortés marches into Tenochtitlan (now Mexico City) with his soldiers and allied natives.

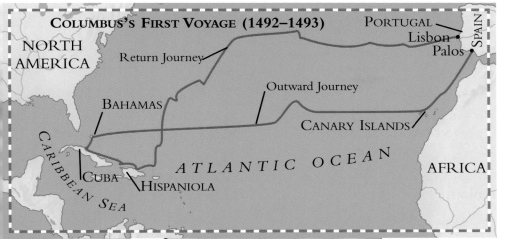

COLUMBUS'S FIRST VOYAGE (1492–1493)

NORTH AMERICA

Return Journey

BAHAMAS

Outward Journey

CANARY ISLANDS

ATLANTIC OCEAN

CARIBBEAN SEA

CUBA

HISPANIOLA

PORTUGAL

Lisbon

Palos

SPAIN

AFRICA

Columbus's first voyage started in Palos, Spain. He stopped for repairs and supplies in the Canary Islands before crossing the Atlantic. The return trip went farther north for favourable westerly winds.

Columbus gave the island its name, which means 'Spanish island'. Locals in canoes helped to unload *Santa María*'s cargo. Columbus ordered a fort to be built on the island and left behind 40 colonists in the new town of La Navidad.

Columbus returned to Spain with his remaining two ships and arrived there in triumph on 15 March 1492. He was awarded the title of Admiral of the Oceans.

Columbus made three more transatlantic voyages, sighting land in Central and South America. On his second trip he discovered that the La Navidad settlers had been massacred by locals. On his third voyage, he was sent back to Spain in chains for misusing his power as governor of Hispaniola but was later found innocent of wrongdoing. His final voyage saw him shipwrecked on Jamaica for a year before he was rescued. He died still convinced that he had reached the coast of Asia.

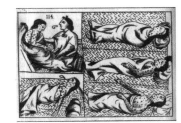

The Spanish conquerors brought diseases to the Americas that nearly wiped out the native populations.

The last Inca ruler, Atahualpa, is captured at the Battle of Cajamarca on 16 November 1532.

Francisco Pizarro
Tempted by tales of Inca wealth, Pizarro and his brothers led three expeditions from Panama into present-day Peru in 1524, 1526 and 1531. After two failures, the third was a success. Pizarro captured the Inca ruler, Atahualpa, at Cajamarca and later had him executed. He took the Inca capital, Cuzco, in 1533 and founded a new city, Lima, in 1535.

Exploring North America
The Spanish began to explore and colonise North America. Juan Ponce de León explored Florida from 1513. He tried, but failed, to establish a colony there in 1521. Hernando de Soto explored southeastern North America from 1539 to 1542 looking for gold and a passage to China.

De Soto reaches the Mississippi River in 1541.

AROUND THE WORLD
1513 – 1769

THE SPANISH DID NOT WANT THE PORTUGUESE TO BE IN CONTROL OF THE SPICE TRADE. IN 1519 AN EXPEDITION FUNDED BY CHARLES I OF SPAIN SET OUT TO FIND A WESTWARD SEA ROUTE TO THE SPICE ISLANDS. LED BY A PORTUGUESE NAVAL OFFICER NAMED FERDINAND MAGELLAN, THE VOYAGE MADE HISTORY BY BEING THE FIRST TO TRAVEL ALL THE WAY AROUND THE WORLD.

Spanish conquistador Vasco Núñez de Balboa reaches the Pacific Ocean in 1513 after crossing the Isthmus of Panama.

After the discovery of the New World, the race was on to continue on to the Indies as Columbus had originally intended. The Spanish explorer Vasco Núñez de Balboa is famous for choosing the site of the first permanent European settlement on mainland America (Darién, in present-day Panama). He was the first to reach the Pacific overland. He crossed from the northern Atlantic coast of the isthmus that makes up Panama to the southern Pacific one.

Ferdinand Magellan set off to find an ocean route in 1519. He and his fleet of five ships sailed around the tip of South America in November 1520.

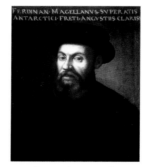

Ferdinand Magellan (1480–1521)

Ferdinand Magellan meets his end on Mactan Island on 27 April 1521. He is killed by local warriors who are loyal to their chief, Lapu-Lapu.

Sir Francis Drake

After the Magellan–Elcano voyage, no European tried to circumnavigate the globe for another 55 years. Then, in 1577, Englishman Francis Drake made the voyage in his galleon the *Pelican*, which he renamed the *Golden Hind*.

Drake was a privateer – a kind of pirate – who raided Spanish treasure ships during his journey.

Francis Drake (above) captures the Nuestra Señora de la Concepción, *a Spanish galleon (right), in March 1579.*

One of his biggest hauls was from a galleon called the *Nuestra Señora de la Concepción*, which was laden with gold, silver and jewels.

When Drake returned to the court of Queen Elizabeth I three years later, she rewarded him with money and a knighthood. During her war against Philip II of Spain, Drake proved himself a hero. His ships carried out raids on Spain and its territories in the Americas. He also helped to defeat the attack of the Spanish Armada in 1588.

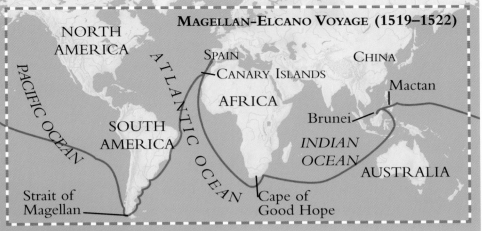

MAGELLAN–ELCANO VOYAGE (1519–1522)

NORTH AMERICA
PACIFIC OCEAN
SPAIN
CANARY ISLANDS
CHINA
ATLANTIC OCEAN
AFRICA
Mactan
SOUTH AMERICA
Brunei
INDIAN OCEAN
AUSTRALIA
Strait of Magellan
Cape of Good Hope

The Magellan–Elcano expedition (1519–1522) travelled west. Victoria was the only one of the original five ships to circumnavigate the globe. It arrived in Spain 16 months after Magellan's death.

Magellan's flagship was a caravel called the *Trinidad*. His other four ships – the *Concepción*, *San Antonio*, *Santiago* and *Victoria* – were larger ships with more room for provisions. Even so, they were not able to carry fresh fruit and vegetables. Many crew died of scurvy, a wasting disease caused by a lack of vitamin C.

Magellan reached the Philippines in March 1521. He converted Rajah Humabon, chief of the island of Cebu, to Christianity. Magellan tried to do the same to Lapu-Lapu, chief of neighbouring Mactan Island, but was killed in the resulting battle. The chief of Cebu lost faith in the Europeans and tried to poison many of Magellan's remaining crew.

The *Victoria*'s commander, Juan Sebastian Elcano, took over as expedition leader. The remaining two ships, the *Victoria* and the *Trinidad*, reached Brunei in June and the Spice Islands in November. They abandoned the *Trinidad* because of a leaky hull.

In the end, only one of Magellan's ships and just 18 of the original 241 crew members made it back to Spain. During their three years away from home, the men had faced countless dangers but also become the first to sail around the world.

William Dampier
English seafarer William Dampier was the first person to sail around the world three times. He made his voyages in 1689–1691, 1703–1707 and 1708–1711. Dampier was also the first European to explore the east coast of New Holland (Australia) in 1699–1701 and describe its unique plants and animals.

William Dampier (above) circled the world three times. On the first of his circumnavigations, he survived being marooned on an island by his crew and later faced a fierce storm in a small canoe (right).

Jeanne Baré
The first woman to circumnavigate the globe was Jeanne Baré – but she had to do so disguised as a man! In those days it was unacceptable for a woman to go exploring. Baré was part of an expedition led by the French admiral Louis Antoine de Bougainville from 1766 to 1769.

On her voyage around the world, Jeanne Baré was assistant to the botanist Philibert Commerson.

THE NORTHWEST PASSAGE
1534 – 1906

MANY NAVIGATORS BELIEVED THERE MUST BE A SEA ROUTE THAT CONNECTED THE NORTHERN ATLANTIC AND PACIFIC OCEANS. LONG BEFORE IT WAS DISCOVERED, THIS ROUTE ACROSS THE TOP OF CANADA AND ALASKA HAD A NAME – THE NORTHWEST PASSAGE. THERE WERE MANY DISASTROUS ATTEMPTS TO PROVE ITS EXISTENCE BEFORE IT WAS FINALLY FOUND.

Jacques Cartier (1491–1557)

The French explorer Jacques Cartier made three voyages to what is now Canada in 1534, 1535–1536 and 1541–1542. He explored the coast of Newfoundland and Gulf of St. Lawrence. He also sailed inland up the St. Lawrence River, which he believed was the fabled Northwest Passage.

English navigator Henry Hudson made two attempts to find the Northwest Passage in the early 1600s. The Hudson River and Hudson Bay are both named after him. In 1611 the crew of his ship, the *Discovery*, mutinied. They abandoned Hudson in a small boat in Hudson Bay.

Henry Hudson, his son and seven crew members are set adrift following a mutiny on the Discovery. None of them are ever heard of again.

In 1819 English naval officer William Parry voyaged almost three-quarters of the way along the Northwest Passage. He turned back when ice began to form as the season changed.

One of the worst disasters was John Franklin's expedition of 1845. His steamships HMS *Erebus* and HMS *Terror* carried contaminated food. The ships became locked in ice, and everyone died, probably of starvation.

In 1854 Irish explorer Robert McClure finally became the first person to cross the Northwest Passage. He travelled by boat and sledge.

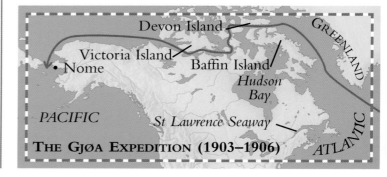

John Franklin (1786–1847)

THE GJØA EXPEDITION (1903–1906)

Roald Amundsen

In 1903 Norwegian explorer Roald Amundsen led an expedition to cross the Northwest Passage in a small fishing boat called the *Gjøa*. He and his five crew learned survival skills from local Inuit people. They reached Nome, Alaska, in 1906.

In 1912 Amundsen became the first person to reach the South Pole, thanks to his use of dog sleds for transport. He also traversed the Northeast Passage (1918–1920) and reached the North Pole (1926).

Roald Amundsen (above) and the Gjøa (right), which is the first ship to cross the Northwest Passage

THE NORTHEAST PASSAGE
1594 – 1880

THE NORTHEAST PASSAGE IS ANOTHER SEA ROUTE THROUGH THE ARCTIC THAT LINKS THE ATLANTIC AND PACIFIC OCEANS. INSTEAD OF GOING AROUND THE TOP OF NORTH AMERICA, IT HUGS THE COASTS OF NORWAY AND RUSSIA, THEN PASSES THROUGH THE BERING STRAIT, A NARROW STRIP OF SEA BETWEEN EASTERN RUSSIA AND THE WESTERN UNITED STATES.

Willem Barentsz dies on his final expedition in search of the Northeast Passage. The Barents Sea is named after him.

The Dutch cartographer and explorer Willem Barentsz went on three expeditions in search of the Northeast Passage in 1594, 1595 and 1596–1597. On the final expedition, Barentsz and his crew became stranded in the ice. They dismantled their ship to build a wooden lodge. The lodge and its contents were discovered in 1871 by a seal hunter.

Portuguese explorer David Melgueiro is said to have sailed across the Northeast Passage in 1660, but there is no proof that he did.

Russian emperor Peter I (1672–1725) funded two expeditions to find the Northeast Passage, both led by naval officer Vitus Bering. The First Kamchatka Expedition (1728–1730) failed due to bad weather.

The Second Kamchatka Expedition (1733–1743) led to the European discovery of Alaska, the Aleutian Islands and Bering Island.

Although the Bering Strait was named after Vitus Bering, he was not the first to pass through it. In 1648 a *Semyon Dezhnev is the first European to sail through the Bering Strait.* Russian soldier named Semyon Dezhnev had sailed around Siberia from the Arctic to the Pacific.

Bering's ships are wrecked on the Aleutian Islands in 1741. Bering dies later the same year, probably of scurvy.

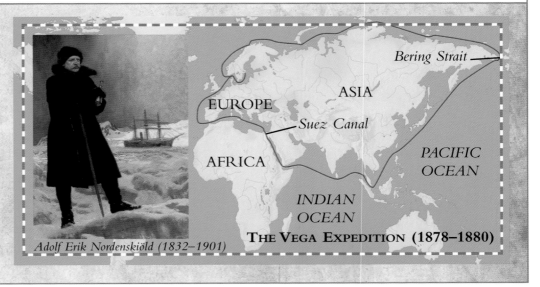

Adolf Erik Nordenskiöld

The Vega expedition was the first to cross the Northeast Passage. It was led by Adolf Erik Nordenskiöld, a Finnish-Swedish geologist who had already taken part in seven expeditions to the Arctic.

The steamship *Vega* set out from Sweden in 1878. It spent most of its first winter icebound in the Bering Strait, then continued on to circumnavigate Eurasia. Its route took it along the newly-built Suez Canal, which had opened a decade earlier.

Adolf Erik Nordenskiöld (1832–1901)

THE VEGA EXPEDITION (1878–1880)

NORTH AMERICAN INTERIOR
1497 – 1806

For the first few hundred years after its discovery, most of North America remained wild and unexplored. Native American peoples continued living undisturbed in the interior, even after Spain, England or France had claimed their lands. It could not last. Slowly, Europeans began to press into the uncharted regions.

John Cabot (around 1450–1498)

King Henry VII of England funded a transatlantic expedition by the Italian explorer John Cabot in 1497. Cabot probably landed in Newfoundland and was the first European to set foot in North America since the Vikings, five centuries earlier.

Others travelled up into the continent from the southwest. In 1540 the conquistador Francisco Vázquez de Coronado set off from Mexico at the head of a huge expedition. It involved hundreds of soldiers and up to 2,000 Mexican Indians.

Francisco Vázquez de Coronado crosses the New Mexico desert in 1540 at the start of his search for the Seven Cities of Gold.

Coronado was looking for New Mexico's cities of gold. They did not exist, but he discovered pueblos inhabited by the Zuni Indians, as well as the Grand Canyon and the Colorado River. Another Spaniard, Hernando de Soto, was exploring the southeast.

Founder of New France and Quebec City, Samuel de Champlain maps the region around the Great Lakes. He makes alliances with Native American peoples, including the Innu–Montagnais, Algonquin and Huron-Wendat.

The Corps of Discovery

In 1803 President Thomas Jefferson bought the Louisiana Territory from France. This vast region, stretching from the Great Lakes to the Mississippi basin, was largely unexplored. Jefferson commissioned an expedition called the Corps of Discovery to map the West. Meriwether Lewis and William Clark led the expedition, accompanied by 30 men, Lewis's slave York and a Shoshoni woman named Sacagawea, who was their guide and translator.

They set out in May 1804 with three boats laden with supplies, trading goods and gifts. They finally reached the Pacific coast in September 1806.

The Corps of Discovery meet Chinook Indians on the Lower Columbia River in October 1805 (above). Lewis, Clark and Sacagawea (right)

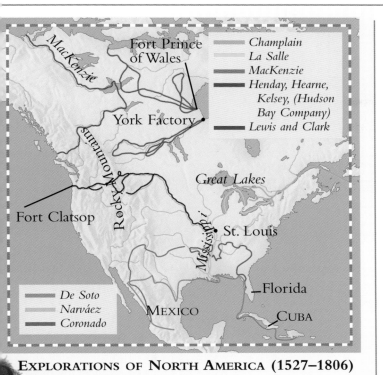

EXPLORATIONS OF NORTH AMERICA (1527–1806)

Map legend:
- Champlain
- La Salle
- MacKenzie
- Henday, Hearne, Kelsey, (Hudson Bay Company)
- Lewis and Clark

- De Soto
- Narváez
- Coronado

Robert de La Salle explores the Great Lakes and Canada. He also travelled the length of the Mississippi, down to the Gulf of Mexico.

De Soto's expedition landed in Florida in 1539. (Florida had previously been explored by another conquistador, Pánfilo de Narváez, in 1528.) De Soto was the first European to cross the Mississippi River.

The French were eager to make their own claims. In 1608 Samuel de Champlain founded New France, an enormous territory that stretched from Newfoundland to the Rocky Mountains and included the Great Lakes. Another French explorer, Robert de La Salle arrived in New France in 1666 and claimed the Mississippi basin for France.

In 1670 the English established a trading post at York Factory on Hudson Bay so that it could control the fur trade north of the Great Lakes. During the 1700s the Hudson's Bay Company funded explorations of the Canadian interior by English adventurers such as Henry Kelsey, Anthony Henday and Samuel Hearne.

The Hudson's Bay Company grows rich selling furs and other resources found by frontiersmen and traders in the Northwest.

Frémont and Walker

The first explorers of the American West also became its first settlers, or frontiersmen. They lived in the mountains and trapped animals for their furs. Some, such as Kit Carson and Joseph Walker, used their knowledge of the frontier to make their names as guides or scouts. They also started particular routes. Walker, for example, established part of the California Trail.

Both Carson and Walker were employed by John Frémont, the 'Pathfinder'. An officer in the US Topographical Corps, Frémont made maps of the West that were useful to settlers and developers. From the 1840s Frémont explored the Oregon Trail and Wind River Range. He travelled from Utah into Oregon and California. He also visited the Sierra Nevada and went up the Missouri, Kansas and Arkansas rivers. Frémont made Walker his chief guide and named the Walker River in his honour.

John C. Frémont (1813–1890)

Joseph Walker (1798–1876)

SOUTH AMERICAN INTERIOR
1541 – 1925

SOUTH AMERICA HAD DEADLY ANIMALS, HOSTILE TRIBES AND DANGEROUS TERRAIN. BUT IT ALSO OFFERED THE PROMISE OF RICHES. THERE WERE EVEN LEGENDS OF A CITY OF GOLD, KNOWN AS EL DORADO. THIS WAS ENOUGH TO SPUR ON THE CONQUISTADORS. BY CLAIMING LAND FOR THEIR KING, THEY HOPED TO WIN HIGHER STATUS AND FINANCIAL REWARDS.

The conquistador Francisco de Orellana set off from the Andes into the Amazon rainforest looking for El Dorado in February 1541. He became the first person to sail along the Amazon River, a distance of 4,000 kilometres (2,500 miles). He arrived at Marajo Island in September 1542. Three years later he returned with a charter from the Spanish king.

The conquistador Pedro de Valdivia founds the Chilean capital city, Santiago, to the east of the Andes Mountains.

It appointed him governor of the region and allowed him to build two cities there. But this expedition was not a success, and Orellana died in the Amazon in 1546.

Pedro de Valdivia had more luck. He arrived in Peru in 1534 to serve the Spanish conquistador Francisco Pizarro. In 1540 he set off from Quito, Peru, to what is now Chile. His force of 150 Spaniards managed to survive the gruelling journey across the Atacama Desert and crush opposition from native Indian peoples. Valdivia founded the city of Santiago in 1541 and later returned to Chile to be its governor from 1549 to 1553.

Fighting off natives and disease, Orellana and his men are the first Europeans to travel the length of the Amazon River.

Map labels: Quito, Pizarro camp, Marajo Island, Amazon, Guayaqua, PERU, BRAZIL, BOLIVIA, CHILE, Santiago

ORELLANA'S ROUTE (1541–1542)

Alexander von Humboldt
Prussian naturalist Alexander von Humboldt travelled in Central and South America from 1799 to 1804.

Humboldt and Bonpland at the base of Mount Chimborazo in Ecuador, which they climbed

Accompanied by his friend, French botanist Aimé Bonpland, he explored the coast of Venezuela, the Amazon and Orinoco rivers and much of Peru, Ecuador, Colombia and Mexico. The pair produced beautiful maps and collected specimens of animals, minerals and around 6,000 plants. Humboldt also discovered the cold ocean current that is responsible for Peru's dry climate. It is now named the Humboldt Current.

Percy Fawcett
No conquistador ever found El Dorado, but the hunt for lost cities boasting ancient wealth continued into the 20th century. English explorer Percy Fawcett disappeared without a trace in Brazil in 1925. He was heading for a city he called 'Z'. The movie character Indiana Jones is based on Fawcett.

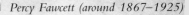

Percy Fawcett (around 1867–1925)

THE SEARCH FOR TERRA AUSTRALIS
1642 – 1779

THE GREEK PHILOSOPHER ARISTOTLE BELIEVED THAT THERE MUST BE A TERRA AUSTRALIS, OR 'SOUTH LAND', TO BALANCE OUT THE CONTINENTS IN THE NORTHERN HALF OF THE WORLD. THIS BELIEF PERSISTED. CENTURIES BEFORE AUSTRALIA WAS EVER SIGHTED, A LAND MASS LABELLED 'TERRA AUSTRALIS' WAS MARKED ON MAPS OF THE WORLD.

James Cook (1728–1779)

English navigator Captain James Cook was sent to explore the Pacific Ocean in 1768. His mission was to go to Tahiti to take measurements as the planet Venus appeared to move across the Sun. After watching this transit of Venus, Cook opened sealed instructions and discovered that he was also to search for Terra Australis.

Aboard HMS *Endeavour*, he mapped the coasts of eastern Australia and New Zealand and claimed Australia for Britain. He named his landing place Botany Bay, because the expedition's naturalists, Joseph Banks and Daniel Solander, gathered so many unique specimens there.

Cook made two more voyages, taking a copy of the new sea watch, H4. Developed by John Harrison, it was the first pocket-sized device for calculating longitude at sea. Cook was attacked and killed in Hawaii in 1779.

Harrison's H4 sea watch

HMS Resolution and Discovery anchor off Tahiti during Cook's final expedition.

Abel Tasman (1603–1659)

Abel Tasman
Cook was not the first to discover Australia. Abel Tasman, an employee of the Dutch East India Company, made two voyages to the region more than a century earlier. On the first, he sighted Tasmania and was then blown off course to New Zealand. On the second, he mapped the north coast of Australia, which he called New Holland.

TASMAN'S AND COOK'S VOYAGES (1642–1779)

HAWAII
Cook killed here
PACIFIC
NEW GUINEA
OCEAN
FIJI · SAMOA · TAHITI
TONGA
AUSTRALIA
Tasmania
NEW ZEALAND

Tasman
1st voyage 1642–1643
2nd voyage 1644

Cook
1st voyage 1768–1771
2nd voyage 1772–1775
3rd voyage 1776–1779

AUSTRALIA
1827 – 1861

JAMES COOK HAD CLAIMED AUSTRALIA FOR THE BRITISH CROWN IN 1770. EIGHT YEARS LATER ARTHUR PHILLIP ARRIVED, THE FIRST GOVERNOR OF NEW SOUTH WALES, A STATE OF SOUTHEAST AUSTRALIA. HE ESTABLISHED A PENAL COLONY THAT LATER GREW INTO THE CITY OF SYDNEY. DURING THE FIRST HALF OF THE 19TH CENTURY, EUROPEANS INVESTIGATED THE REST OF AUSTRALIA.

Around 15,000 spectators watch the Burke and Wills expedition set off from Royal Park, Melbourne, on 20 August 1860.

Captain James Stirling explored the Swan River area of what is now Western Australia in 1827. He returned to England with news of its fertile lands. Two years later the Swan River Colony was set up. It was the first colony in Australia for ordinary settlers, not criminals. But the land was not as good for farming as Stirling had thought. Although the colony survived, it was not as successful as those in New South Wales.

In 1859 the South Australian government offered a reward for the first successful south–north crossing of the continent west of the 143rd line of longitude. Hoping to win the reward, Irishman Robert O'Hara Burke and Englishman William John Wills led an expedition from Melbourne up to the Gulf of Carpentaria. They took 26 camels with them, as well as 23 horses and six wagons. However, they had competition. Scottish explorer John McDouall Stuart was also heading up into northern Australia.

Burke and Wills sight the Gulf of Carpentaria.

Charles Sturt

Naval officer Charles Sturt arrived in Sydney in 1827. He was transporting convicts on his ship, the *Mariner*. The Governor of New South Wales asked him to explore the interior of Australia. On his first expeditions, Sturt charted the waterways of New South Wales. In 1835 he settled in the region to start a farm. He went on a third expedition in 1844 in search of an inland saltwater lake. He reached the barren deserts of northwestern New South Wales.

Sturt leaves Adelaide in South Australia to explore northwestern New South Wales.

Burke, Wills and King return to the camp on Cooper Creek on 21 April 1861, exhausted. They find supplies there, but the rest of the party left just hours earlier.

In November 1860, Burke and Wills left some men and supplies at Cooper Creek (up until then, the northernmost point of European exploration). They continued on to Camp 119 with two men, John King and Charles Gray, and then into the mangrove swamps of the Gulf of Carpentaria. However, the journey back was horrific. Gray died of dysentery, and the others almost starved. By the time they reached Cooper Creek, the rest of the party had given up on them, leaving just a few buried provisions. Rescue teams were sent out, but they failed to find the men. Wills and Burke died in June 1861. Only King made it back to Melbourne.

Between 1858 and 1861, John McDouall Stuart had led five expeditions into the centre of Australia. In October 1861 he set off on a sixth. He finally reached the northern coast near present-day Darwin on 24 July 1862. In 1871–1872, Australia's Overland Telegraph Line was built along his route.

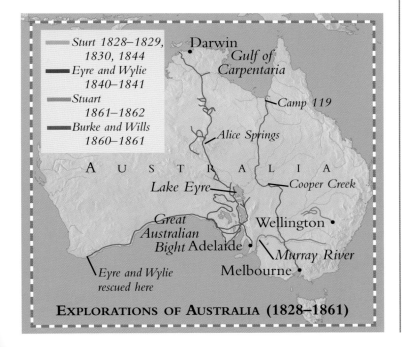

Legend:
- Sturt 1828–1829, 1830, 1844
- Eyre and Wylie 1840–1841
- Stuart 1861–1862
- Burke and Wills 1860–1861

EXPLORATIONS OF AUSTRALIA (1828–1861)

John McDouall Stuart (above); planting the first telegraph pole (right)

Eyre and Wylie

Edward John Eyre explored South Australia. In 1839 he left Adelaide with Irish explorer John Baxter and three Aboriginals, Yarry, Joey and Wylie. However, when supplies ran low, Yarry and Joey shot Baxter and ran off with most of the food. Eyre and Wylie continued. When they completed their 3,200-km (2,000-mile) journey to Western Australia, they were in a sorry state. Luckily they were rescued by a whaling ship, the *Mississippi*.

Eyre and Wylie are rescued by a whaling ship near Esperance, Western Australia.

INTO AFRICA
1795 – 1894

DURING THE PERIOD OF THE SLAVE TRADE, PORTUGAL, HOLLAND, FRANCE, SPAIN AND BRITAIN HAD ESTABLISHED TRADING POSTS ON THE WEST AFRICAN COAST. HOWEVER, FEW EUROPEANS TRAVELLED INTO THE INTERIOR OF SUB-SAHARAN AFRICA. THAT ALL CHANGED IN THE 19TH CENTURY. EXPLORERS RACED TO SHED LIGHT ON THE MYSTERIOUS 'DARK CONTINENT'.

Heinrich Barth approaches Timbuktu in 1853.

Heinrich Barth was one of the first Europeans to travel into Africa. Along with the astronomer Adolf Overweg, a fellow-German, Barth joined an expedition led by the English explorer James Richardson in 1849. After Richardson and Overweg died of diseases, Barth continued on alone. Already fluent in Arabic, he met with African chiefs and historians and learned their languages too. He heard about the powerful Songhai Empire that had flourished in Mali in the 1400s and built the great cities of Timbuktu and Djenné. In 1857 Barth published a scholarly book about his travels in both German and English, which was illustrated with his own sketches.

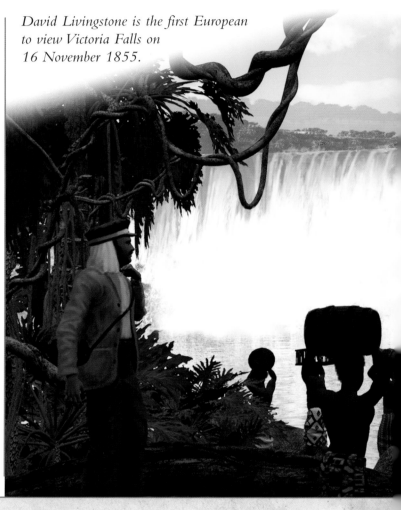

David Livingstone is the first European to view Victoria Falls on 16 November 1855.

Mungo Park (1771–1806)

Mungo Park
Scottish explorer Mungo Park left England on the *Endeavour* in May 1795. That December he set out from a British trading post up the Gambia River with just two local guides. He traced the central section of the Niger River for about 500 km (300 miles).

In 1805 Park headed a larger expedition to the interior, made up of nearly 50 people. Many died of dysentery before they even reached the Niger River. Only Park and a handful of men went beyond Timbuktu. They were drowned after their boat struck a rock and was attacked by hostile locals.

Capelo and Ivens
Portuguese explorers Hermenegildo Capelo and Roberto Ivens led an expedition into southern central Africa in 1877. They travelled from Angola on the west coast to Mozambique in the east, exploring the Zambezi River and reaching Victoria Falls. They returned to explore the region again from 1884 to 1885. This time they were able to set up a west–east overland trade route.

Capelo and Ivens

AFRICAN EXPLORATIONS (1794–1894)

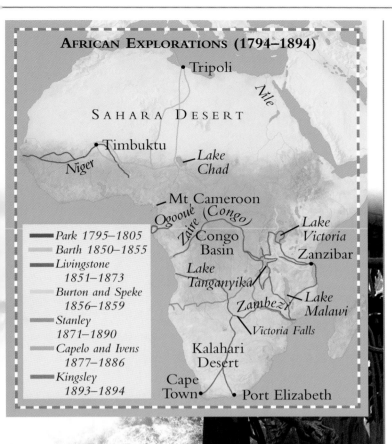

- Tripoli
- SAHARA DESERT
- Nile
- Timbuktu
- Niger
- Lake Chad
- Mt Cameroon
- Ogooué
- Zaïre (Congo)
- Congo Basin
- Lake Tanganyika
- Lake Victoria
- Zanzibar
- Zambezi
- Lake Malawi
- Victoria Falls
- Kalahari Desert
- Cape Town
- Port Elizabeth

- **Park 1795–1805**
- **Barth 1850–1855**
- **Livingstone 1851–1873**
- **Burton and Speke 1856–1859**
- **Stanley 1871–1890**
- **Capelo and Ivens 1877–1886**
- **Kingsley 1893–1894**

Burton (carried on a litter because he is too ill to walk) and Speke (blinded by illness) discover Lake Tanganyika in 1858.

While Barth was exploring western Africa, the Scottish missionary and doctor David Livingstone was travelling around central and southern Africa. He mapped the Zambezi and saw Victoria Falls. Livingstone wanted to bring Christianity and trade to Africa and end slavery. He also wanted to find the source of the Nile River. When he disappeared in the 1860s, an American journalist named Henry Stanley found him at Lake Tanganyika and greeted him with the words, "Dr. Livingstone, I presume?"

The lake had been discovered in 1858 by two Englishmen, Richard Burton and John Speke. Like Livingstone, they wanted to know where the Nile began. Setting off from Zanzibar, they spent four years exploring Africa's great lakes. During the journey Speke became the first European to see Lake Victoria.

Stanley finds Livingstone on 10 November 1871 near Lake Tanganyika.

Female explorers in Africa

Exploration was a man's world in the 19th century, and the long dresses that western women wore at that time did not help. But a few female pioneers had a thirst for adventure. Dutch explorer Alexandrine Tinné travelled around northeastern and central Africa in the 1860s. In 1869 she set out to cross the Sahara Desert. Tinné would have been the first woman to do so. However, she was murdered along the way for reasons that cannot be confirmed.

Englishwoman Mary Kingsley was inspired by tales of David Livingstone. In the 1890s she went up the Congo and Ogooué rivers. She lived with the Fang people, ignoring rumours that they were cannibals. She also became the first non-African woman to climb Mount Cameroon.

Mary Kingsley (1862–1900)

Alexandrine Tinné (1835–1869)

DESERTS OF ASIA AND ARABIA
1894 – 1935

IN THE 19TH CENTURY, DETERMINED EUROPEANS SET OUT TO MAP THE LAST UNCHARTED PARTS OF CENTRAL ASIA AND ARABIA (THE MIDDLE EAST). THEY CROSSED SNOW-CAPPED MOUNTAINS AND BURNING DESERTS AND WROTE ABOUT THE PEOPLE AND LANDSCAPES THEY ENCOUNTERED.

Starting in the 1890s, the Swedish explorer Sven Hedin made four expeditions into the mountains and deserts of central Asia and China. He became an expert on Turkestan and Tibet and also mapped the Great Wall of China in the deserts of the Tarim Basin. Hedin was working on behalf of the Russian emperor, who was hoping to extend Russia's borders into central Asia. Great Britain feared Russia was a threat to its own empire in India. It sent explorers into the region too.

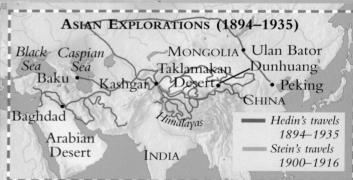

Aurel Stein with his dog Dash and the rest of his team at Ulugh-Mazar, a ruined settlement in the Tarim Basin, in 1908.

The Hungarian explorer Aurel Stein worked for the British and was a rival of Hedin's. Stein also made four journeys into central Asia. During his first, he discovered Dandan Oilik, an abandoned town in the Taklamakan Desert. In 1907 Stein found the famous 'Caves of the Thousand Buddhas' near Dunhuang, China. They contained the world's oldest printed book, the *Diamond Sutra* (868 AD).

Hedin nearly dies of thirst in the Taklamakan Desert in 1895. He carries water in his boot back to fellow-traveller Kasim.

ASIAN EXPLORATIONS (1894–1935)

Black Sea • Caspian Sea • Baku • Kashgar • MONGOLIA • Ulan Bator • Taklamakan Desert • Dunhuang • Peking • CHINA • Baghdad • Himalayas • Arabian Desert • INDIA

━━━ Hedin's travels 1894–1935
━━━ Stein's travels 1900–1916

The Arabian deserts

At the beginning of the 20th century, parts of Arabia belonged to the Ottoman Empire (present-day Turkey). Writers and diplomats such as TE Lawrence (better known as Lawrence of Arabia) and Gertrude Bell explored the region and knew its people. They supported the Arabs when they revolted against Ottoman rule in 1916.

Two world wars moved the borders in the Middle East. Wilfred Thesiger was one of the first westerners to explore the Arabian Desert after World War II. He crossed it twice in the late 1940s. Thesiger also lived with the marsh Arabs in Iraq, whose way of life had not changed in thousands of years.

Wilfred Thesiger (1910–2003)

Gertrude Bell (1868–1926)

JUNGLES OF INDOCHINA
1858 – 1933

INDOCHINA IS THE NAME FOR THE REGION EAST OF INDIA AND SOUTH OF CHINA. GREAT CIVILISATIONS HAD ARISEN HERE IN EARLIER TIMES, BUT DURING THE 19TH CENTURY, MOST OF IT WAS PART OF THE FRENCH OR BRITISH EMPIRES. TODAY THIS MAINLAND AREA OF SOUTHEAST ASIA IS MADE UP OF CAMBODIA, LAOS, MALAYSIA, BURMA, THAILAND AND VIETNAM.

Cambodia is home to Angkor Wat, the largest temple complex in the world. The Khmer people built it in the 12th century. It began as a Hindu temple, but when the Khmer converted to Buddhism, so did the temples.

Angkor Wat was known about in the West, but not widely. Then French explorer Henri Mouhot visited the site in 1860. He was on a three-year expedition into Siam, Cambodia and Laos to collect specimens of jungle plants and insects. Over three weeks Mouhot made detailed drawings of the temple

Mouhot and his guides approach Angkor Wat through the trees.

HENRI MOUHOT'S EXPLORATIONS (1858–1861)

complex and wrote vivid descriptions of the buildings. His work helped to fire up people's imaginations and make Angkor Wat popular in the West. Mohout incorrectly believed that an earlier people had constructed the complex. He thought it too beautiful to be the work of the Khmer people who were still living in Cambodia. Mouhot died of malaria in 1861 during his fourth expedition in the area.

one of Mouhot's drawings of Angkor Wat

Eugène Dubois

The jungles of Southeast Asia also held treasure for the Dutch anthropologist Eugène Dubois. Between 1887 and 1895, he dug at several sites on the Indonesian islands of Sumatra and Java. This led to his discovery of a fossil of an early human – one of the first hominids found outside Africa or Europe.

Dubois discovered a Homo erectus, nicknamed 'Java Man', on Java in 1891.

Michael Leahy

Australian explorer and photographer Michael Leahy is famous for discovering the Highlands of Papua New Guinea in the 1930s. Leahy's

Leahy is filmed just before he climbs into his plane to explore the Wahgi Valley in the Papua New Guinean Highlands.

photos and films revealed Papua New Guinea's native people and their culture and customs to the world.

SCIENTIFIC EXPLORATION
1799 – 1969

GREAT EXPEDITIONS THROUGHOUT HISTORY HAVE INCLUDED SCHOLARS OR SCIENTISTS. THESE MEN AND WOMEN HAVE PUT THEMSELVES IN GREAT DANGER IN ORDER TO COLLECT SPECIMENS OF ROCKS, PLANTS AND ANIMALS OR ARCHAEOLOGICAL TREASURES. THEIR FINDS HAVE ADDED TO OUR UNDERSTANDING OF THE WORLD – ITS PEOPLE AND ITS GEOGRAPHY.

The naturalist Joseph Banks accompanies James Cook on his first voyage.

His feet briefly on firm land again, Darwin sets off to collect flora and fauna on one of the Galápagos Islands.

Charles Darwin (1809–1882)

British naturalist Joseph Banks visited three continents besides Europe during his career. In 1766 he visited Newfoundland and Labrador in North America and documented their plants and animals. Next, he joined James Cook aboard HMS *Endeavour*. He employed other botanists to help collect specimens, as well as artist Sydney Parkinson to record their finds. During the voyage, which stopped at Brazil, Tahiti, New Zealand and Botany Bay in Australia, Parkinson made nearly 1,000 drawings of plants and animals.

Naturalist Charles Darwin might never have made his name if he hadn't joined the survey ship HMS *Beagle* as a companion to its captain, Robert FitzRoy. It was the ship's second voyage, and for nearly five years, it was kept busy surveying the coasts of southern South America, the Galápagos Islands, Tahiti and Australia.

Under the ocean

Explorers have sailed across the ocean since prehistoric times. The ability to explore the region under the ocean is more recent. The first successful submarine was built in 1620 by Dutchman Cornelius Drebbel for military use. William Beebe and Otis Barton's bathysphere was for observing deep-sea creatures in their natural habitat. It could be lowered 920 metres (3,028 feet).

The first self-propelled submersible was Auguste Piccard's bathyscaphe in the late 1940s. French marine biologist Jacques Cousteau built his own version in the late 1950s and nicknamed it the *Diving Saucer*. It even had a grabber for collecting specimens.

In 1960 Piccard's son Jacques piloted the bathyscaphe *Trieste* to the deepest part of the oceans, 10,911 metres (35,800 ft) down in the Pacific.

Beebe and Barton with their bathysphere in the 1930s

Cousteau's Diving Saucer

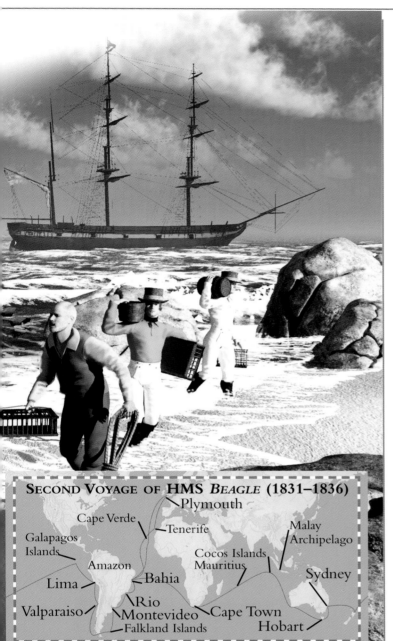

During his years in the Amazon (1848–1859), Bates sends home specimens of nearly 15,000 species.

The samples that Darwin took, and the plants and animals that he observed, helped him to develop his theory of evolution by natural selection. This was the idea that species could give rise to new ones over time, because individuals with characteristics that suited a changing environment would be more likely to reproduce.

Two of Darwin's supporters in the scientific community were the naturalists Alfred Wallace and Henry Bates. Wallace came up with the idea of natural selection independently from Darwin. He backed up his ideas with fieldwork in the Amazon (with Bates) and the Malay Archipelago. Bates's time in the Amazon helped him to notice animal mimicry – for example, harmless butterflies having the same warning colours as poisonous ones or hoverflies looking like wasps.

Inhabitants of the Aru Islands in the Malay Archipelago help Wallace with his specimen collection by shooting at greater birds-of-paradise.

SECOND VOYAGE OF HMS *BEAGLE* (1831–1836)

Plymouth
Cape Verde
Tenerife
Galapagos Islands
Malay Archipelago
Amazon
Cocos Islands
Mauritius
Bahia
Sydney
Lima
Valparaiso
Rio
Montevideo
Cape Town
Falkland Islands
Hobart

Piccard (centre) and Don Walsh (left) in the Trieste

Thor Heyerdahl

In 1947 Norwegian adventurer Thor Heyerdahl sailed across the Pacific Ocean on a simple raft called the *Kon-Tiki*. The total distance covered was around 8,000 km (5,000 miles). Heyerdahl wanted to show how ancient people could have made long sea voyages.

In 1969, Heyerdahl built a papyrus boat, *Ra*, based on sources from ancient Egypt. His first attempt to cross the Atlantic from Morocco failed, but he succeeded in *Ra II*.

Heyerdahl's raft, the Kon-Tiki, *in the Pacific*

ENDS OF THE EARTH
1893 – 1959

THE POLES WERE TWO OF THE LAST FRONTIERS OF EXPLORATION. AS WELL AS FREEZING TEMPERATURES, THE NORTH POLE POSED AN ADDITIONAL CHALLENGE. IT LIES IN THE ARCTIC OCEAN, WHERE MOST OF THE SEA IS FROZEN ALL YEAR ROUND.

Nansen and Johansen leave the Fram *on 14 March 1895 and set off across the Arctic ice.*

The Norwegian adventurer Fridtjof Nansen designed his ship the *Fram* to cope with Arctic conditions. When it hit ice, its hull bobbed up instead of being crushed. Nansen took the *Fram* on its first voyage to the Arctic Ocean in 1893.

Two years later the *Fram* took Nansen and a companion, Hjalmar Johansen, north before they continued by dog sled. Bad weather forced the two men back, but they came close to success – within 380 km (240 miles) of the North Pole.

Swedish engineer Salomon Auguste Andrée hoped to cross the North Pole in a different means of transport – a hot-air balloon. In 1893 and 1896 he carried out test flights. In 1897 he set off with fellow-Swedes Knut Fraenkel (also an engineer) and Nils Strindberg (a photographer). The balloon crashed after just two days. Badly prepared, the men set off on foot toward a supplies depot at Cape Flora but never reached it. The men's dead bodies were found in 1930. Despite finding diary notes of the expedition, experts disagree whether they died of starvation, cold, disease - or perhaps polar bears!

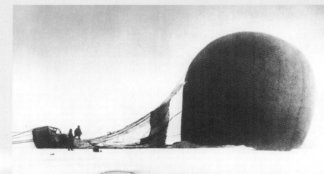

Strindberg took this photo of Andrée and Frænkel at the site of the balloon crash.

Race to the South Pole

Two rival expeditions arrived in Antarctica in early 1911, each with its sights set on the South Pole. One was led by British naval officer Robert Falcon Scott - the other by the Norwegian, Roald Amundsen.

Scott's expedition relied on ponies and motor sleds, which could not cope with the extreme cold and had to be shot or abandoned. Amundsen's team had all dogs, which were suited to the environment.

When Scott reached the pole, he discovered that Amundsen had beaten him there. His team began to make their way back on 19 January, but they were too weak. By the end of March, they were all dead.

Scott's group at the South Pole, 17 January 1912

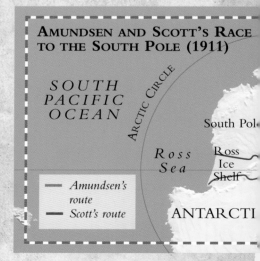

AMUNDSEN AND SCOTT'S RACE TO THE SOUTH POLE (1911)

SOUTH PACIFIC OCEAN

ARCTIC CIRCLE

South Pole

Ross Sea

Ross Ice Shelf

— Amundsen's route
— Scott's route

ANTARCTI

US naval officer Robert Peary was desperate to be first to reach the North Pole. After two failed attempts, he had one last try in 1908, reaching the North Pole with his assistant, Matthew Henson, on 6 April 1909. Rival explorer Frederick Cook argued he had reached the pole a year earlier, but was shown to be lying.

Robert Peary (1856–1920)

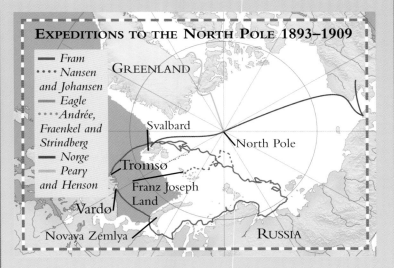

EXPEDITIONS TO THE NORTH POLE 1893–1909

— *Fram*
···· *Nansen and Johansen*
— *Eagle*
···· *Andrée, Fraenkel and Strindberg*
— *Norge*
— *Peary and Henson*

GREENLAND
Svalbard
North Pole
Tromsø
Franz Joseph Land
Vardø
Novaya Zemlya
RUSSIA

Umberto Nobile looks out of an observation window (left) during the 1926 transpolar flight of the Norge.

The first aircraft to fly over the North Pole was the *Norge* in 1926. The airship, whose name meant Norway, was built and piloted by Umberto Nobile, an Italian aircraft engineer. Norwegian explorer Roald Amundsen led the expedition. American naval officer Richard E. Byrd falsely said that he had beaten them to it but, like Cook, had his claims dismissed.

In 1958 the nuclear submarine USS *Nautilus* became the first submarine to reach the North Pole. USS *Skate* arrived at the North Pole about a week later, on 11 August 1958, commanded by James F. Calvert. Neither ship could break through the pack ice because it was too thick. However, USS *Skate* made another attempt the following year. On 17 March 1959 USS *Skate* succeeded in becoming the first submarine to surface at the North Pole.

USS Skate *surfaces at the North Pole on 17 March 1959.*

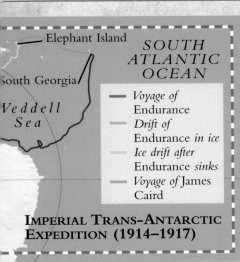

— Elephant Island
South Georgia
Weddell Sea

SOUTH ATLANTIC OCEAN

— *Voyage of Endurance*
— *Drift of Endurance in ice*
— *Ice drift after Endurance sinks*
— *Voyage of James Caird*

IMPERIAL TRANS-ANTARCTIC EXPEDITION (1914–1917)

Shackleton and the *Endurance*
Irish explorer Ernest Shackleton came within 160 km (100 miles) of the South Pole in 1909. But he had to turn back because of bad weather and low supplies. He tried to reach the pole again in 1914. That expedition was not a success either. After their ship the *Endurance* was crushed by pack ice, Shackleton and his men took three lifeboats to nearby Elephant Island. Then Shackleton left his men there and took his lifeboat, the *James Caird*, 1,300 km (800 miles) to South Georgia, where there was a whaling station. From there he was able to arrange a rescue.

Shackleton died of a heart attack in 1922 while on one last expedition.

launching James Caird *from Elephant Island*

GLOSSARY

archipelago
A chain or large group of islands.

astrolabe
A navigation instrument used at sea to measure the height of the Sun at midday in order to work out a ship's latitude.

botanist
A scientist who studies plants.

cartographer
Someone who makes or draws maps.

circumference
The distance around a circle or sphere. The circumference of Earth at the equator is 40,075 km (24,900 miles).

circumnavigate
To travel all the way around something.

colony
A region or country that is controlled by another country. People who settle in a colony are called colonists.

conquistador
A Spanish soldier and explorer who came to the Americas in the 1500s.

continent
One of Earth's seven great landmasses: Europe, Asia, Africa, North America, South America, Australia and Antarctica.

cross-staff
An early navigation instrument used at sea to measure the angle of a celestial body, such as the Moon or the Pole Star, from the horizon in order to work out a ship's position.

Crusade
One of a series of military expeditions from Christian Europe to recover the Holy Land from Muslim rule. The first Crusade took place in 1096–1099. The Crusades ended in 1291 with the fall of the last Crusader castle at Acre.

dugout
A canoe hollowed out from a tree trunk.

dysentery
A disease that causes severe diarrhoea.

evolution
The process by which living things gradually change over very long periods of time and that gives rise to new species.

geographer
A scientist who studies Earth's surface, climate, peoples and resources.

geologist
A scientist who studies rocks and minerals.

isthmus
A narrow strip of land that connects two larger areas of land.

land bridge
A connection between landmasses that people and animals can travel across to move from one to the other. Rising sea levels have submerged land bridges that were usable in prehistoric times, such as those beneath the Bering Strait and English Channel.

latitude
Imaginary horizontal lines that circle Earth and are measured in degrees north or south of the equator. Navigators calculate latitude to determine how far north or south they are.

longitude
Imaginary vertical lines that circle Earth and are measured in degrees east or west of a line called the Greenwich Meridian, which passes through London, UK. Navigators calculate longitude to determine how far east or west they are.

longship
A sailing ship with oars used by Viking sea raiders.

marooned
Left behind on a desert island.

missionary
A person who travels abroad to convert the local people to his or her religion. The place where a missionary settles is called a mission.

native
A person or other living thing born or originating in a particular place.

natural selection
A process that favours the survival of living things that are best suited to their surroundings and makes them more likely to pass on their genes (instructions for life). Charles Darwin was the first to fully describe it, and it is the driving force of evolution.

naturalist
A scientist who studies natural history – all species of living things including plants and animals.

navigation
The science of finding the right direction to travel by using maps and other equipment.

outback
The remote, rural parts of Australia.

penal colony
A colony where criminals are sent to live out their lives as punishment. The first British settlements in Australia were penal colonies.

privateer
A person who has legal authority to raid enemy merchant ships and take a share of what they find.

pueblo
A Native American town or village in the southwestern United States, where homes are usually built of stone or adobe mud.

scurvy
A disease of the skin and gums caused by lack of vitamin C. Seafarers often suffered from it, because they did not eat enough fresh fruit and vegetables.

Silk Road
The ancient trading route between China and Europe. Merchants carried Chinese silks and spices along it to Europe.

slave
Someone who is owned by someone else and has to work for them.

slave trade
The transatlantic trade in slaves that went on between the 15th and 19th centuries. European ships traded their goods for captured African slaves. They transported the slaves to colonies in the Americas to work on huge farms called plantations or as servants.

submersible
A boat that can travel underwater for research or exploration.

trade
The process of buying and sellling goods.

transatlantic
Across or on both sides of the Atlantic Ocean.

tribute
Payment from one people or country to another, more powerful one as a sign of respect.

INDEX